1982

The National Poetry Series

The National Poetry Series was established in 1978 to publish five collections of poetry annually through five participating publishers. The manuscripts are selected by five poets of national reputation. Publication is funded by James A. Michener, Edward J. Piszek, The Ford Foundation, The Witter Bynner Foundation, and the five publishers—Doubleday, E. P. Dutton, Harper & Row, Random House, and Holt, Rinehart and Winston.

THE NATIONAL POETRY SERIES — 1981

George Barlow, *Gumbo* (Selected by Ishmael Reed)
Larry Levis, *The Dollmaker's Ghost* (Selected by Stanley Kunitz)
Robert Peterson, *Leaving Taos* (Selected by Carolyn Kizer)
Michael Ryan, *In Winter* (Selected by Louise Glück)
Reg Saner, *So This Is the Map* (Selected by Derek Walcott)

IN
WINTER

IN WINTER

Michael Ryan

HOLT, RINEHART and WINSTON
New York

Published by Holt, Rinehart and Winston, 383 Madison Avenue, New
York, New York 10017.
Published simultaneously in Canada by Holt, Rinehart and Winston of
Canada, Limited.

Library of Congress Cataloging in Publication Data
Ryan, Michael, 1946-
  In winter.
  (The National poetry series)
  I. Title. II. Series: National poetry series.
PS3568.Y39I5   811'.54   80-19799
ISBN Hardbound: 0-03-058942-6
ISBN Paperback: 0-03-058941-8

First Edition

Designer: Constance T. Doyle

Printed in the United States of America
10 9 8 7 6 5 4 3 2 1
These poems appeared originally in the following publications:

American Poetry Review: The Pure Loneliness, Wet Streets, In Winter,
Memory; *Antaeus*: Poem at Thirty, Sex; *The Atlantic Monthly*: Gangster
Dreams; *Harper's*: A Changed Season; *The Nation*: A Quick Day in the
Country; *The New Republic*: An Apology to Patty; *The New Yorker*:
Consider a Move; *Ploughshares*: All the Time, Where I'll Be Good, Why,
You Can Thank; *Poetry*: After, An Old Story, A Shape for It, Hopeless,
Stones, The Black Hole, The Great Dark, To Tell You the Truth, Waking
at Night, When I Was Conceived; *Poetry Now*: 1976. "The Pure
Loneliness" also appeared in *The Pushcart Prize II* and is dedicated to
John Skoyles; "Waking at Night" is dedicated to Louise Glück; "In
Winter" is for Jacqueline Vaught. Thanks to the National Endowment
for the Arts, to Yaddo, and to the Vermont Council of the Arts for their
support.

Contents

V

* This symbol is used to indicate a space between stanzas of a poem wherever such spaces are lost in pagination.

I

Poem at Thirty

The rich little kids across the street
twist their swings in knots. Near me,
on the porch, wasps jazz old nesting tunes
and don't get wild over human sweat.
This is the first summer of my middle life.
I ought to be content. The mindless harsh
process of history, with its diverse murders
and starvations, its whippings, humiliations,
child-tyrants and beasts, I don't care for
nor understand. Nor do I understand
restlessness that sometimes stops my sleep.

Waking, those mornings, is like being thrown from a train.
All you know comes to falling:
the body, in its witless crooning for solidity,
keeps heading for the ground.
There is no air, no sound, nothing
but dumb insistence of body weight
coming down, and there is no thought of love,
or passing time, or don't want to be alone.
Probably one hundred thousand impressions
wrinkle the brain in a moment like this,
but if you could think about it
you'd admit the world goes on in any case,
roars on, in fact, without you, on its endless iron track.

———

But most mornings I ease awake:
also a falling,
but delicate as an agile wing
no one may touch with hands,
a transparent wing like a distant moan
arriving disembodied of pleasure or pain,
a wing that dissolves on the tongue,
a wing that has never flown.

Because I've awakened like this
I think I could love myself quietly
and let the world go on.

So today I watched a pudgy neighbor
edge her lawn, and heard the small blade whine;
I saw her husband, the briefcase man,
whiz off in his Mercedes without a glance.
I believe I'm beginning to understand
that I don't know what such things mean—
stupid pain or pure tranquillity,
desire's dull ache or conquering the body,
the need to say we and be known to someone
or what I see in myself as I sit here alone.

The sun glares most mornings
like an executive's thick pinky diamond,
and slowly the dark backs off.
This is one reason this morning I awakened.

———

No one can tell you how to be alone.
Some fine people I've known swirl to me
in airy forms like just so much hot dust.
They have all moved through in dreams.
A lover's smell, the gut laugh of a friend,
become hard to recall as a particular wind.

No one can tell you how to be alone.
Like the deep vacuum in sleep, nothing
holds you up or knocks you down, only
it doesn't end in waking but goes on and on.
The tangles of place, the floating in time,
you must accept gently like a favorite dream.

If you can't, and you don't, the mind
unlocks the mind. Madness, with his lewd grin,
always waits outside the window, always
wanting to come in. I've gone out before,
both to slit his throat and kiss his hand.
No one can tell you how to be alone:

Watch tiny explosions as flowers break ground;
hear the children giggle, rapid and clean.
It's hard to care about ordinary things.
Doesn't pain expand from lack of change?
I can't grasp exactly the feelings of anyone.
No one can tell you how to be alone.

———

At thirty the body begins to slow down.
Does that make for the quiet on this porch,
a chemical ability to relax and watch?
If a kid bounces her pelvis against a chain-link fence,
bounces so metal sings
and it seems she must be hurting herself,
how old must I get before I tell her to stop?

Right now, I let her do it.
She's so beautiful in her filthy T-shirt
and gym shorts, her hair swings with each clang,
and she can do no wrong.
I let her do it as background music
to storm clouds moving in like a dark army.
I let her do it as a fond wish for myself.
I feel the vibration of the fence
as a wasp feels voices on a pane of glass.
The song in it I can't make out.

This day, then, ends in rain
but almost everyone will live through it.
Tomorrow, mad with need, a widow
in Angola might dynamite the consulate
or feed her children to the pigs.
Maybe the sun's first light will hit me
in those moments, but I'd gladly wake to feel it:
the dramatic opening of a day,
clean blood pumping from the heart.

II

Seven Annihilations and a Slight Joke

Stones

They don't change, or change so slowly
only the dead could notice.
Because the dead don't feel death
pulse inside the body like a white ocean
that consumes all possible attention,

an ocean whose quiet bottom cradles
the odd undersides of stones,
while hard wind shakes up everything
above. If stones won't feel
even the final storm,

if the dead really notice nothing,
how will you feel yourself
becoming something else
when the only thing
that ignores the crash of waves
is stone?

The Black Hole

The black hole from which nothing comes
and in which men slide like night deposits
opens now its metal mouth for you,
bored and mechanical: still, rank absence,
whatever you call it,
doesn't affect at all the daily flatness;
no one loses himself for a moment
in this immense impersonal orifice
because even dumbbells know what hurts
and the black hole, whatever you call it,
hurts. So life goes on quietly desperate,
as in a crazed magnate
expertly relishing the coldness of cash,
but no matter where you go you take up too much space.

To Tell You the Truth

Like a thin rock spinning across a lake
(with luck, it ends up on a meager beach;
without luck, it sinks): no one penetrates.

If sister touches herself in the mirror
of that lake, if brother stops and sees her,
what choice but embarrassment or insane desire?

Look at yourself watching them, so distant
and lonely. You feel your own grief
when you hold another's grieving body.

But just as the fingertip knows the lush touch,
just as the thin rock slaps the water back
as hard as the hand that threw it,

in the deepest part of yourself
there is no one to tell you the truth.

Hopeless

All this endless unconnected desire
all this clumsy bumping each other
always out of the old habit of fear

Nothing inside but the absence of nothing
nothing to want but want still happens
on this night without whispers or screams

If only no one hoped for a thing
if touch for instance were perfect connection
a goodbye kiss might seem a gift

and a stiff wind a nice surprise
and mean talk just stroking the throat
and death itself merely sullen and constant

An Old Story

Like an old story's need for detail
each time retold, the syntax
twisting through it like tails in water,

what's needed now's another timely lover
to make love touchable as a tight curve.
Her syntax does the tricks: her animal parts

move beyond herself, you think, as you feel
knee gliding always to thigh, and wind about
the solid geometry of breasts.

If you also realize *she doesn't need me*
when you come to her brain living alone
like a queen, and that you to her are only

another lover, remember even love obeys laws
of time and need, and like a simple wave
rises to its height, breaks, and is over.

The Pure Loneliness

Late at night, when you're so lonely
your shoulders lean to the center of your body,
you call no one and you don't call out.

This is dignity. This is the pure loneliness
that made Christ think he was God.
This is why lunatics smile at their thoughts.

Even the best moment, as you slip
half-a-foot deep into someone you like,
sinks to the loneliness in it
through the loneliness that's not.

If you believe in Christ hanging on the cross,
his arms spread as if to embrace
the Father he calls who is somewhere else,

you still might hear your own voice
at your next great embrace, thinking
loneliness in another can't be touched,

like Christ's voice at death answering himself.

After

The space we feel inside us
is the space a survivor sees
as he swims endlessly toward a place

where he might put his feet down
and take an easy breath. For now,
the sheer distance means a long time

he must hurt himself enough
to tow his own weight and not give up.
Why, he asks in each stroke,

and in each stroke pain is felt,
muscles do their work, and he thinks
of no one else. Is this what's meant

when we look into ourselves
and feel nothing but the urge to go on?
The sun goes down. He sees nothing.
It's calm.

The Great Dark

Before anything else,
before the first animal
stumbled over a rock

in the first dim light
and growled under its breath,
there was The Great Dark.

The Great Dark never talked.
The Great Dark only danced
about itself, inside and out,

and when from the energy of that
long dance something else showed up,
The Great Dark slipped away and sulked.

III

Sex

After earth finally touches the sun,
and the long explosion stops suddenly
like a heart run down,
the world might seem white and quiet
to something that watches it in the sky all night,
so something feels small,
and feels nearly human pain.

But it won't happen again:
the long nights wasted alone, what's done
in doorways in the dark by the young,
and what could have been for some.
Think of all the lovers and the friends!
And in the middle of everything, a man
still turns to himself as to a wall,
leaning completely into a stiff rough wall.

Sex eased through everyone,
even when slipping into middle age
as into a lover's skin,
and prying out again to find
the body slumped with flesh, muscles gone,
and bones readied for the turn to dust.
Then no one minds when one lover
holds another, like an unloaded sack.
But the truth enters at the end of life.
It enters like oxygen into every cell,
and the madness it feeds there in some
is only a lucid metaphor
for something long burned to nothing,
like a star.
*

No one gets over his desire.
No one hurries out of each desire,
like ponderous clothes, one at a time,
until what's underneath is known.
We knew genitals as small things
and we were ashamed they led us around,
even if the hill where we'd lie down
was the same hill the universe unfolded upon
all night, as we watched the stars,
when for once our breathing seemed to blend.

————

Each time, from that sweet pressure
of hands or the great relief of the mouth,
a person can be led out of himself.
Isn't it lonely in the body?
The myth says we ooze about as spirit
until there's a body made to take us,
and only flesh is created by sex.
That's why we enter sex so relentlessly,
toward the pleasure that comes
when we push down far enough
to nudge the spirit rising to release,
and the pleasure is pleasure of pure spirit,
for a moment all together again.
So sex returns us to beginning, and we moan.

————

Pure sex becomes specific and concrete
in a caress of breast or slope of waist:
it flies through itself like light, it sails
on nothing like a wing, when someone's there
to be touched, when there's nothing wrong.

So the actual is touched in sex,
like a breast through cloth: the actual
rising plump and real, the mind
darting about it like a tongue.
This is where I wanted to be all along:
up in the world, in touch with myself . . .

Sex, invisible priestess of a good God,
I think without you I might just spin off.
I know there's no keeping you close,
as you flick by underneath a sentence
on a train, or transform the last thought
of an old nun, or withdraw for one moment alone.
Who tells you what to do or ties you down!

I'd give up the rest to suck your dark lips.
I'd give up the rest to fix you exact
in the universe, at the wildest edge
where there's no such thing as shape . . .

What a shame I am if, reaching the right woman
in a dim room, pure sex holds itself apart
from us like an angel in an afterlife,
and with the ideas no one has even dreamed
it wails its odd music for pure mind.

———

After there's nothing,
after the big blowup of the whole shebang,
what voice from what throat
will tell me who I am? Each throat
on which I would have quietly set my lips
will be ripped like a cheap sleeve
or blown apart like the stopped-up
barrel of a gun. What was inside them
all the time I wanted always
to rest my mouth upon?

I thought most everything
stuck dart-like in the half-dome of my brain,
and hung there like fake stars in a planetarium.
It's true that things there changed into names,
that even the people I loved were a bunch of signs,
so I felt most often alone.
This is simply the way we live and nothing to bemoan.
We know it the first time we extend an arm:
the body reaches so far for so long,
we grow and love to grow, then stop, then lie down.

I wanted to bear inside me this tender outcome.
I wanted to know if it made sex happen:
does it show up equally in touch and talk?
does it leak from the mind, as heat from the skin?
I wanted my touching intelligent, like a beautiful song.

IV

When I Was Conceived

It was 1945, and it was May.
White crocus bloomed in St. Louis.
The Germans gave in but the war shoved on,
and my father came home from work that evening
tired and washed his hands
not picturing the black-goggled men
with code names fashioning an atomic bomb.
Maybe he loved his wife that evening.
Maybe after eating she smoothed his jawline
in her palm as he stretched out
on the couch with his head in her lap
while Bob Hope spoofed Hirohito on the radio
and they both laughed. My father sold used cars
at the time, and didn't like it,
so if he complained maybe she held him
an extra moment in her arms,
the heat in the air pressing between them,
so they turned upstairs early that evening,
arm in arm, without saying anything.

Wet Streets

There is no mention of them
in this report I make to you
that says it is so awfully possible
to love many people at one time.
Needless to say, it rains enough
some nights to slip out of myself
entirely into sadness, as if sadness
acts as another beautiful woman
who mentions not the slightest demand.

So this doesn't mention demands,
and I don't even talk about the streetlights
whose reflections, and the shadows
they make, really are dangerous.
If I could look once at the source
of myself, I might describe
a purely impersonal place
where we all touch, and tell you
the common history of our bodies
as if exclusion were as unnatural
as the awful sound of single drops of rain
leaking into this empty building
that keeps making sense by itself.

Consider a Move

The steady time of being unknown,
in solitude, without friends,
is not a steadiness which sustains.
I hear your voice waver on the phone:

Haven't talked to anyone for days.
I drive around. I sit in parking lots.
The voice zeroes through my ear, and waits.
What should I say? There are ways

to meet people you will want to love?
I know of none. You come out stronger
having gone through this? I no longer
believe that, if I once did. Consider a move,

a change, a job, a new place to live,
someplace you'd like to be. *That's not it,*
you say. Now time curves back. We almost touch.
Then what is? I ask. What is?

Waking at Night

I won't die in my sleep.
My sorry entrance into absence,
that featureless space, will be made
as I awake, fumbling deep for breath
as for a key suddenly misplaced.
That featureless space:
like an endless level field of ice
where the eyes whiten,
where invisibles fidget like gnats . . .

I suspect hell is white,
the soul wandering constantly,
calling out for company, while the wind
blows through it as if it were nothing.
And what does the body know
now, sleeping through its nights alive?
It knows it will be left behind.

It knows it will be left behind
the way a lover knows the ending's coming.
Think of those you've loved and touched
and never seen again. Sometimes I wake
at night inside this thought, and stumble
through the dark to call someone
and say *I miss you, I feel your loss.*

I won't die in my sleep.

You Can Thank

If you sneeze into a towel
you can thank the fluffed cotton
for not being steel
you can thank the cotton boll
for not thinking how to grow

but growing anyhow through hard
flatpacked deep south dirt
in one slow-motion explosion
from seed not out but up
up in a stiff upward thrust

you can thank the cotton gin
and the man Eli Whitney
a name you got wrong
on the final history exam
you can thank the third grade nun

for the softness of her veils
as she pinned you in the clothes closet
the cold crucifix her breathy whisper
thank Jesus O thank Jesus
everywhere your body muffled in cloth

1976

Sometimes, from wanting too long,
a man hears the impeccable cry from inside
that says all life he knows goes wrong.
Then he hurts himself mowing the lawn,
or flings an end table through the television screen,
or fingers warm Scotch on the porch by himself
while watching the neighbor's shingles shed rain.
He might begin a wild lifetime feud
with an old friend by the simple movement of his hand.
He might gather his small family around him
in the den, and be unable to say a thing.

This cry doesn't come from the land
that's gangbanged by rabid capitalists
and returned, like a bruised girl, to her friends.
This cry doesn't come from the ancestors
who walked with axes over their shoulders
to Arkansas from British Columbia,
whose gentleness is forgotten, whose desire
and courage impress briefly, like new movies.
This cry comes from inside,
where the beauty of a country is exact,
and the necessary profitable interconnectedness
among all citizens could not mean less.

Where I'll Be Good

Wanting leads to worse than oddity.
The bones creak like bamboo in wind,
and strain toward a better life outside the body,
the life everything has that isn't human.

Feel the chair under you? What does it want?
Does lust bend it silly like a rubber crutch?
Tell a tree about the silky clasp of cunt.
It won't shift an inch. It won't ache to touch.

Let me not cruise for teens in a red sports car,
or glare too long at what bubbles their clothes.
Let me never hustle file clerks in a bar.
Keep me from the beach when the hot wind blows.

If I must go mad, let it be dignified.
Lock me up where I'll feel like wood,
where wanting can't send me flopping outside,
where my bones will shut up, where I'll be good.

In Winter

At four o'clock it's dark.
Today, looking out through dusk
at three gray women in stretch slacks
chatting in front of the post office,
their steps left and right and back
like some quick folk dance of kindness,
I remembered the winter we spent
crying in each other's laps.
What could you be thinking at this moment?
How lovely and strange the gangly spines
of trees against a thickening sky
as you drive from the library
humming off-key? Or are you smiling
at an idea met in a book
the way you smiled with your whole body
the first night we talked?
I was so sure my love of you was perfect,
and the light today
reminded me of the winter you drove home
each day in the dark at four o'clock
and would come into my study to kiss me
despite mistake after mistake after mistake.

A Shape for It

Sometimes when time goes by
I feel it bend.
The day becomes the same white room,
and the day won't end.

Its walls show no human scratch,
no useless wild attempt,
and echo no curse or cry,
but do not relent.

I wake amazed to be inside,
like an inmate slapped awake
while dreaming of an endless field
where the sun makes

festival of a girl's long yellow hair,
and she sways to gather
her dress as she waits,
and time seems clear as air.

Gangster Dreams

Who made gangster dreams?
　The old moss on the brain.
Who calls to you upstairs?
　One in winter without a fire.
Who won't listen to you talk?
　I don't listen. You can't talk.
What's that face in the bedroom mirror?
　That's the gangster. He's the gangster.

What's trapped beneath the cellar?
　That's the gangster underwater.
Where's the house wrapped in fire?
　No one's house with no one there.
What slim victim cries for air?
　That's the gangster. He's the gangster.
Who made gangster dreams?
　The old moss on the brain.

All the Time

Intimate agonies should be wordless as birds,
small dull birds in dark scary woods,
but they don't care how they talk
or what beasts inside they become to break out.
The wind through those woods grows with them,
humming all night beneath hearing
like wire inside a building,
a wind pressing so gently
you'd think it understands.

It doesn't understand.
What you are and have been
forms the same answerless question,
the same relentless question bending you down
into a quiet resigned old man, while inside's
all pecking and screeching and mad flapping wings.
It happens all the time. Gravity in time
means flesh loosens and hangs, so the skeleton
emerging seems to say *this is what I am, it's what
I've always been.*
                At least that is the illusion.

A Changed Season

The tree has given its brief fruit
and the wind comes on with its weird caress.
Now, without stars, night seems limitless
like shadows of shadows over the earth.

She wanted to hold for one slim moment
leaves as they opened, the tree
unfolding its thin arms like a cripple
wheeled out for his afternoon sun.

But after any touch what stays on?
Wind, tree, or tongue, delicate and warm?
Better she curl in her own dark warmth
than try to go where they have gone.

An Apology to Patty

I'm sorry for telling you why I am sad
the nights we lie wide-eyed
in bedroom darkness. It might be the fact
you can become afraid at what I say
and press next to me, your right hand
flat above my heart, your left arm
tucked under like a wing,
that makes me say it again
as the solid familiar objects of the room
rise from shadow to outline
like animals coming out of the ocean.
If I could still see them
when the light goes off and the air
suddenly blackens,
I might not be overtaken
by this sense that the life I've chosen
is the wrong one
and tell you, as if then
you could take it inside you
and so take me along.

A Quick Day in the Country

1.

The mountains, in the thick morning mist,
look like huge beasts waiting for life,
but they're still mountains and nothing else.
I don't believe I seem anything to them:
not the wrong husband, not a hard man,
not the man who'd love to need no one,
not a person whose loving causes harm.

2.

Where are those trees where we always met,
because there, maybe in only shaded light,
I would watch the shadows hollow your face
and believe I felt inside your life and death,
but I haven't since we left, and this afternoon
I'd like to know where those trees are,
although it's not a place I'd be by myself.

3.

This day will always stay quiet,
like an old woman long ruined by love.
Although the trees seem to complain
when the wind makes them dance all night
like a pack of rooted ghosts, I'll not speak
again. If I could, though, I'd tell you
her story, and that she had to love him.

Memory

It's like watching an underwater show
through glass, where girls share
an air hose and ride huge fish.
My father drove us to see it
in the new '56 Buick, his gaudy Florida
shirt tattoed to his chest with sweat,
while we kids whaled on one another
in the back, read road signs and whined
in concert until his backhand swung
blindly over the top of the seat,
clipping the unlucky one caught in its arc
and that one would cry quietly to himself
while for five minutes the rest of us shut up.

Now, in this overlay of silences,
my father dead, me at my mother's house
for a brief visit, I recall our lives
seemed perfectly on the surface,
even if my sister had nervous attacks
and we were warned about strange men
who would try to pick us up.
Of course we are taken along by events
without grasping what's happening
until later when memory gives them shape
that may not encompass the facts.
But today I see my whole childhood
in the curves and flutterings of the girls
who had learned to smile while holding
their breath, and though it must be only
a reflection on the glass, behind them
I see my father drowning in the tank.

V

Why

I wish I could walk deep into a field
of spiked wheat reaching my waist
and not ask that question,
where the sun laces my chest
with its indifferent heat, and the sky
seems only a backdrop for sharp birds
that tuck their wings and glide,
where each step pops crickets into quick arcs
like bingo balls in the glass air machine
an old man sits to watch at evening
and does not ask that question
of himself, or of anyone near him.

Because why can land you in prison.
Why can walk you to a traffic island
where you find yourself for no reason.
Why can enter your dreams like a demon
and you wake up the next morning
not the same.
                        It always starts this way,
breeding inside until it swarms into things,
blackening the sky, in chorus with wind . . .

Tonight, in summer, cornered in my room,
jamming my hard feelings into a wordless song
that has hummed for centuries snagged in the genes
and now pokes out of my particular brain
into these words, taut as a thorn,
and demands a brief life of its own,
*

so, too, I want to be done
lugging through the gloom,
and wish I could walk deep into a field,
stretch out my joined limbs, and hold on.

———

Conscious in darkness, the lost thoughts
almost heard, like whispering in the distance:
I click off my light, watch the pines
sway with their own weight—
huge furred arms motioning *come on*
with the swish and caress of black waves.

Who has not watched the ocean at night
and heard its old invitation?
That same dusky word licks through the pines.
I press my face against the screen
and remember I did this exact thing
as a child on my grandmother's farm
waking one night to roam the house alone.
There was something out there I didn't know,
in the shadows, under the deep black trees,
something that wanted me. I wouldn't go to it
for anything, but suddenly even the house
seemed strange, and I felt it touch me
all over like cold air after a shower.
Afraid, I squeezed behind the ancient radio
and spent the night. It became a family joke.

Was there a moment then I could have known
why the world shoves us away while taking us in?
That question needles my brain like a germ.

———

Who gives a shit about carcajou
in the boscage, or pansies freaked with jet?
I'd like to write a daylight poem
that pretends the world's a good friend,
but what relation to things makes a link
that won't snap with all the shaking it gets?

In this thick dark the room seems blank
like a man long dead and forgotten.
I can't stop the draining of the days.
But when night edges in, and bad panics hum
like light-drunk bugs diving at the screen,
it still brings sweet expectations of return.

And what pleasure comes just lying in the sun,
or talking intensely, or loving someone—
what pleasure enters, private as a dream,
rushing through the body from the slightest thing,
through the nooks and caverns, bouncing like sound,
until it fades to whispers, and then it's gone.

Outside, the great pines face a black sky.
What can be named that is close and stays?
I know the silence of an empty house
can greet at the door with an amazing smack.
I don't want to hear what keeps me apart
when I whirl my one dance toward the large.

———

What first word first rounded out a mouth?
And what dumb animal spoke it?

Like a child who sings himself to sleep,
the brain turns to itself at night
because the delicious burnish of things
melts into the dark.
                    So now I write
about loneliness, how it pockets me inside it,
and the longing to be freed from it
I always walk around with.

It doesn't matter that now it's summer
and the breeze might let me forget
if I could lie here naked and blank,
because breeze comes easy as a sexless kiss
and breeze won't plant me finally
outside myself, and that is what I want.

Still it pleases me to think of you
reading this in another time and place,
at another chance axis of those old infinites,
while I sit in this green chair in Massachusetts,
while I think even at this moment we orbit,
even at this moment we wave past
with a faceless prehistoric minding-our-business
which is neither desperate nor malicious,
like two similar beasts at a brief distance
when the whole world was a forest.

ABOUT THE AUTHOR

In Winter is Michael Ryan's second volume of poetry. His first book, *Threats Instead of Trees*, won the Yale Series of Younger Poets Award and was nominated for a National Book Award in 1974. His essays on poets and poetics have been published in *American Poetry Review, Antaeus,* and *Poetry.* He has taught poetry and literature at the University of Iowa (where he earned his M.F.A. and Ph.D. and also served as an editor of *The Iowa Review),* Southern Methodist University, the M.F.A. Writing Program at Goddard College (which he directed in 1978–79), and most recently, at Princeton University.

Every step is certain in Michael Ryan's second collection of poems; they are written with passion and exacting poetic economy. In his descriptions of love and sex, of the desperation and hope in solitude, he also outlines the mystery of intelligence: its awareness of its own inadequacy within the physical world, a world that comes to us in immediate, sensual forms, in palpable images that shift as rapidly as thought itself, in words that combine to make a profound and beautiful music.

In Winter was selected for The National Poetry Series by Louise Glück, author of three collections of poems: *Firstborn*, *The House on Marshland*, and *Descending Figure*.